THE STORY OF JOHN LEWIS

A Biography Book for New Readers

Written by
Tonya Leslie, PhD

Illustrated by
Jerrard K. Polk

ROCKRIDGE PRESS

Dedicated to changemakers everywhere, whose "good trouble" makes the world better.

For general information on our other products and services or to obtain technical support, please contact our Customer Care Department within the United States at (866) 744-2665, or outside the United States at (510) 253-0500.

Rockridge Press publishes its books in a variety of electronic and print formats. Some content that appears in print may not be available in electronic books, and vice versa.

Series Designer: Angela Navarra
Interior and Cover Designer: Julie Schrader
Art Producer: Sue Bischofberger
Editor: Eliza Kirby
Production Editor: Jenna Dutton

Illustration © 2020 Jerrard K. Polk. Maps courtesy of Creative Market.

Photography © ClassicStock/Alamy Stock Photo, p. 51; Paul Schutzer/The LIFE Picture Collection/Getty Images, p. 53; and kropic/iStock.com, p. 54.
Author photo courtesy of Christina Morassi.

ISBN: Print 978-1-64876-697-8 | eBook 978-1-64876-194-2
R0
Printed in China

CONTENTS

CHAPTER 1

A HERO IS BORN

Meet John Lewis

When John Lewis was a young boy, he was in charge of the chickens on his family's farm. He cared for them all and even named them! When he got older, he became a **civil rights** leader and a US **congressman**. He spent most of his life speaking out against **injustice**. John Lewis was raised in an unfair America. When he was young, **Black** and white people lived separately and unequally. John spent his life fighting to change that, but he fought peacefully. When people yelled, John stayed silent. While others raised their fists, John lowered his hands. When people yelled out bad words, John sang out freedom songs.

It is not easy to stand up for peace, especially when others act with violence. John knew that fighting for **equality** was dangerous. He was beaten, kicked, and spat upon. He was jailed more than 40 times. Still, he stood his ground. He held on to his belief that people should be treated equally. People around the world watched his bravery, and they joined in to help.

John Lewis never stopped fighting for justice, and he never stopped believing in peace.

John's America

John Lewis was born on February 21, 1940, in a small farming community in Alabama. He lived near the city of Troy. He came from a big family.

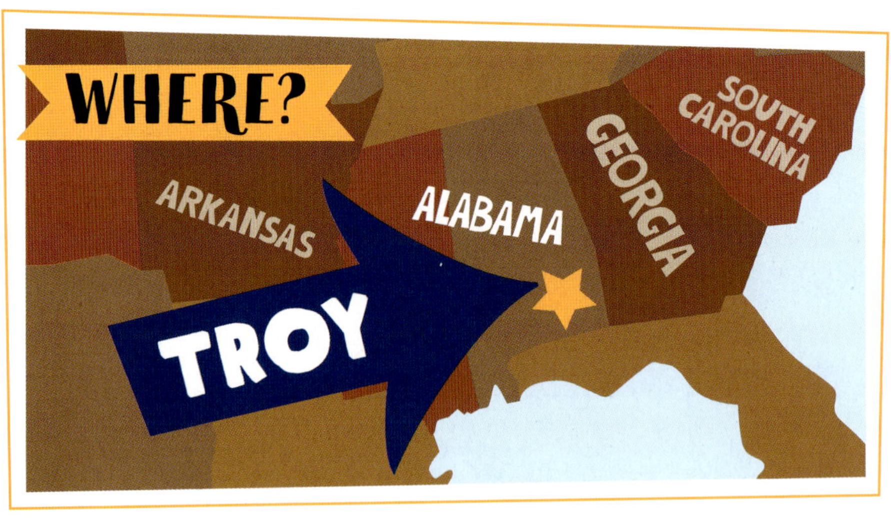

He was the third of 10 children. Most of his neighbors were family, too. John spent his early life never meeting a stranger.

John's family had worked on the land since the days of **slavery**. White Americans in the South **enslaved** Black people and forced them to work for free. After slavery ended in 1865, many laws and unfair practices were put in place to keep Black people down. One unfair practice was **sharecropping**. White landowners

JUMP —IN THE— THINK TANK

John always wanted to be fair. How do you practice fairness with your friends and family?

rented land to Black farmers. Then, at the end of the growing season, they shared the harvest. But the white landowners often took more than their fair share. They left the farmers with almost nothing. No matter how hard the Black farmers like John's family worked, they barely made enough to live on.

Black and white people lived separate lives. Their children went to different schools. There were some places Black people

couldn't go at all. When John tried to go to the library, he was told that it was for white people only. This was called **segregation**.

MYTH & FACT

MYTH: If sharecroppers worked harder, they could have made it.

FACT: Sharecropping was unfair and racist. Even when Black farmers tried to fight back, the laws protected the white landowners.

Even as a child, John could see that this way of life was unfair. John decided that he needed to fight for a better world.

WHEN?

1865 — Slavery ends.

1896 — "Separate but equal" becomes law.

1940 — John Lewis is born.

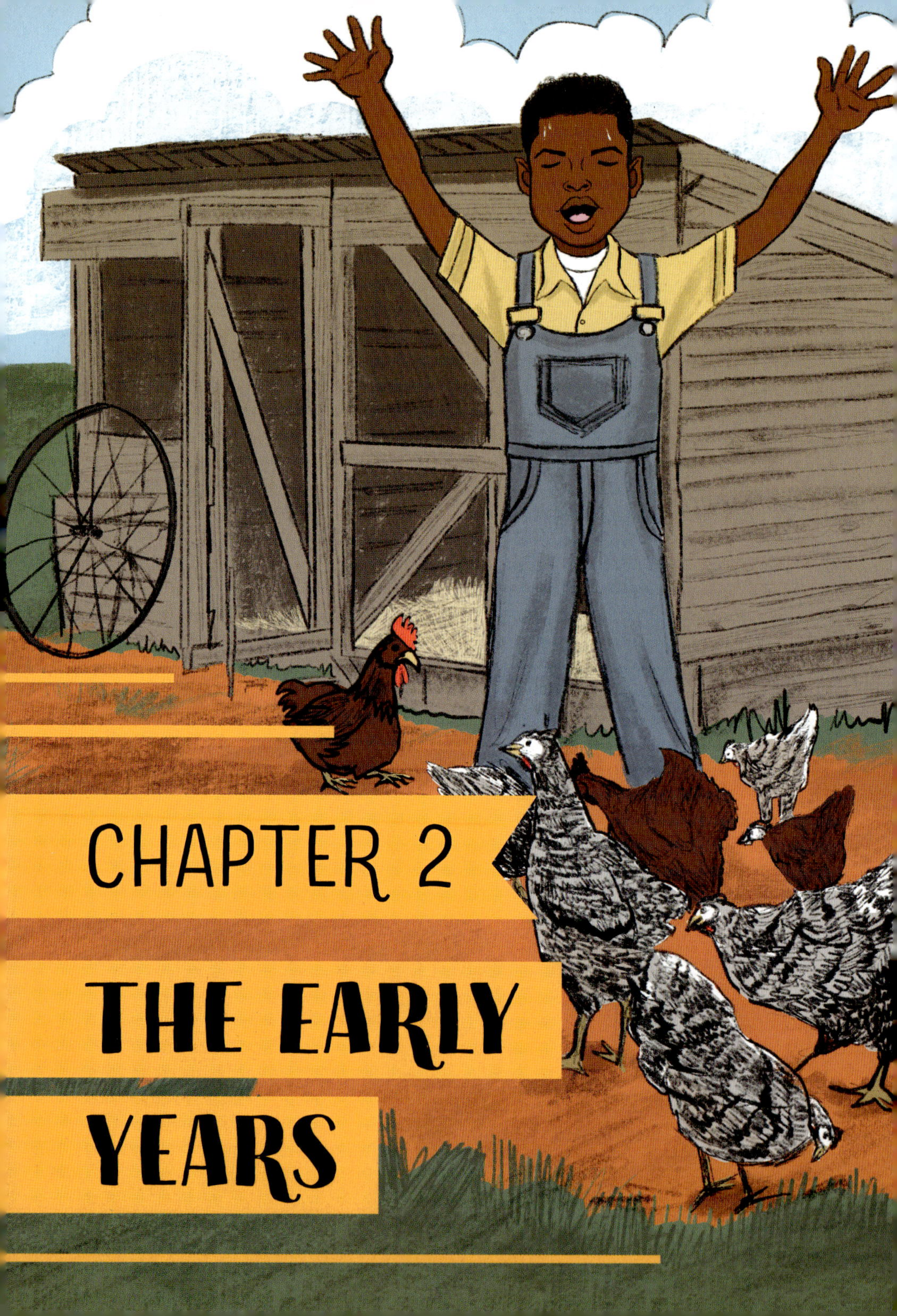

CHAPTER 2

THE EARLY YEARS

Preaching to the Chickens

John's parents, Eddie and Willie Mae, eventually bought a farm of their own. Now John's family had 110 **acres** of land. They planted cotton, corn, and peanuts. They also had their own animals. Farming was hard work for the whole family, and everyone had to do their part.

John's job was to take care of the chickens. He had to feed them and make sure their eggs were kept warm and safe. John felt a special connection to the chickens. John wanted to be a **pastor**, so sometimes he preached to them. Some nodded their heads. Others looked at John with curiosity. The chickens couldn't talk, but John knew they were listening.

Besides the chickens, John also loved school. But there was a lot of work on the farm. Sometimes John and his brothers and sisters needed to stay home to help.

The Lewis Family

John begged to go to school. He told his family how far he would fall behind. His parents felt bad, but they had no choice. Everyone had to help out.

One morning, John had an idea. He hid under the front porch and waited. When he saw the school bus coming down the road, he rushed from his hiding place and ran to the bus. He got on and went to school. John's parents weren't happy. But they didn't punish him. They knew how much he liked school. This was John's first protest.

JUMP IN THE THINK TANK

John had to choose between working on the farm and going to school. Have you ever had to make a hard choice?

Separate Is Not Equal

John didn't know many white people when he was growing up. He was used to segregation. When he went to school, he saw that white children rode on a newer bus and had a better school building. Even though he loved his school and his teachers, this didn't seem fair. John would ask his family why things were this way. They would say, "That's just the way it is."

Then, one day John went on a trip to Buffalo, New York, with his uncle Otis. They were going to visit family who lived in the North. As they drove through the Southern states, they didn't stop much. They couldn't. Because of segregation, they were not allowed in some of the restaurants they passed. They could get **harassed** or hurt. So John and Otis ate in the car.

Things were different in Buffalo. John noticed that his uncles there had white neighbors. White and Black people sat together and were friends.

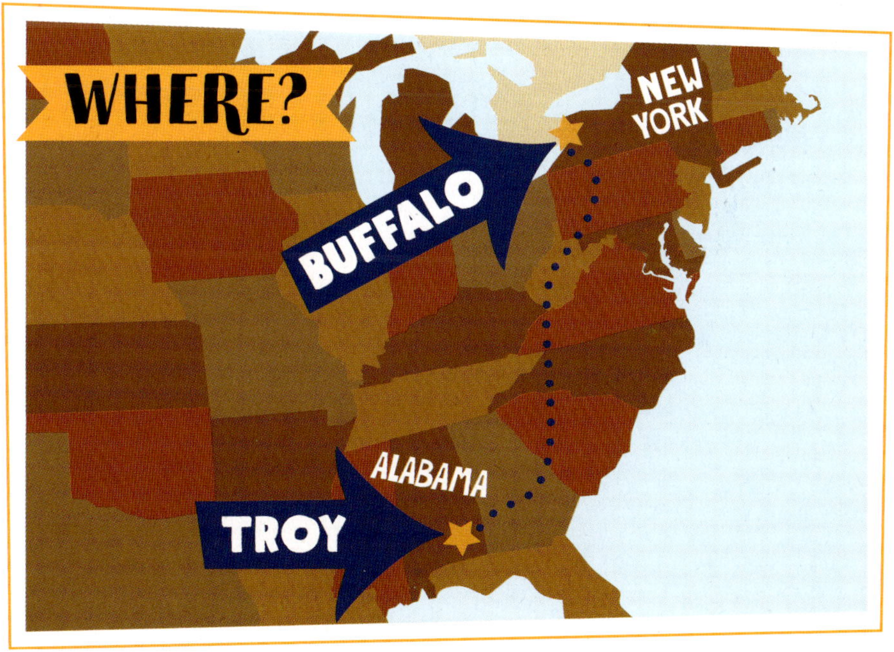

John realized that segregation didn't have to be the way things were.

All around, the world was changing. In 1954, a big decision was passed in the courts. It was called *Brown versus Board of Education*. In the decision, the court said that schools could no longer be segregated. John was excited! He thought this meant that he would be able to go to a better school.

But change didn't come right away. In fact, a lot of things got worse. In 1955, a 14-year-old boy named Emmett Till was murdered in Mississippi. His crime? Talking to a white woman.

MYTH & FACT

MYTH: After the Brown court decision, Black and white children went to school together right away.

FACT: It took many years and a lot of hard work to **desegregate** schools.

No one was punished for his murder. Emmett's mother was so hurt and angry. She decided the world needed to see what was done to her son. A funeral photo of Emmett was published in a magazine. People couldn't believe what they saw. The country was **outraged** about his murder. John was, too. He wondered how he could make a difference.

John heard a speech by a pastor named Dr. Martin Luther King Jr. and was inspired. He thought that if he became a preacher, he could reach people. Maybe he, too, could fight for change like Dr. King.

WHEN?

1951	1954	1955
John visits Buffalo, NY.	*Brown v. Board of Education* ends school segregation.	Emmett Till is murdered.

CHAPTER 3

TIME TO TAKE A STAND

Faith and Courage

School segregation was finally against the law. But other types of segregation continued. Black and white people still couldn't eat in the same restaurants. In parts of the South, Black people had to ride in the backs of buses. If a white person wanted a seat, Black passengers had to stand up. In 1955 in Montgomery, Alabama, Rosa Parks refused to stand up to let a white man sit down. This act of courage sparked a yearlong bus **boycott**. The Montgomery Bus Boycott was America's first large protest for civil rights.

Meanwhile, John pushed for change in his own way. He preached his first public sermon. The audience was filled with people, not chickens! Because he was only 15 years old, the story was covered in the newspaper.

Then he learned about a school in Nashville, Tennessee, called the American Baptist Theological Seminary. It helped Black people become ministers. John applied and was accepted after high school. The school was far from home. He had to work hard to pay for his classes. He loved learning, but he wanted to help his community. He wanted to fight for justice.

Then John had an idea. He would apply to Troy University. It was a good school and close to his family. If he went to Troy, he could move home. But Troy didn't allow Black students.

John wanted to desegregate the school. He knew he couldn't do it alone, so he wrote to ask Dr. King for help. Then he waited. One day he got a letter from Dr. King. The minister wanted to meet John!

☆ The Boy from Troy ☆

John went to Montgomery to meet Dr. King. When he got there, Dr. King asked, "Are you the boy from Troy?" He had read the newspaper article about John's sermon. John couldn't believe Dr. King already knew who he was!

Dr. King wanted to help John desegregate the university. They would need lawyers, and it would cost money. It was also dangerous. John could get hurt. His family could lose their jobs. Their homes might be bombed. It had happened before.

John thought about it the whole ride home. What should he do?

John talked to his family. They wanted to support him, but they were worried. John did not want to put them in danger. So he wrote to Dr. King. It was a hard choice, but he would not try to desegregate Troy University after all. Instead, he went back to school in Nashville. John was disappointed. But he didn't know that this decision would change his life forever.

John met a man named James Lawson Jr. James taught people about nonviolent protest. **Nonviolence** means working for change peacefully.

MYTH & FACT

Myth: Being nonviolent is easy.

Fact: Staying nonviolent takes a lot of practice. It is especially hard when other people are being violent.

Rosa Parks started a nonviolent protest when she would not give up her seat. John liked the idea of nonviolence. He couldn't imagine

JUMP IN THE THINK TANK

Do you think nonviolent protests are a good idea? Why or why not?

hurting anyone. He didn't even want to hurt his chickens! But nonviolence is not easy, especially when others are violent toward you.

John met other students who wanted to use peace to fight for change. They were men and women, Black and white. They decided to desegregate the **lunch counters** in their town. They practiced for months. Finally, they were ready to act!

WHEN?

1955	1956	1957	1958
The Montgomery Bus Boycott starts.	John preaches his first public sermon.	John goes to school in Nashville.	John and Dr. King meet.

CHAPTER 4

PEACEFUL PROTESTS

Lunch Counter Sit-Ins

John and the other students were ready to launch their first peaceful protest. They organized a **sit-in**. The plan? They would sit down at a lunch counter. Then, when workers refused to serve them, they would not leave. They would just sit quietly until the store closed. The next day, they would come back and do it again.

At first, the white store owners were confused. Then they got mad. They tried to get the protestors to leave. They yelled horrible things and tried to pull them off the stools. They beat John and the others, and dumped food on their heads. The police came. But they arrested the protestors! It was John's first arrest.

Even though John and other protestors were in jail, the sit-ins continued. When other students heard what happened, they came out to protest, too. Eventually, they formed an organization called the Student Nonviolent Coordinating Committee (SNCC).

Three lawyers agreed to help John and the others at no charge. When the protestors got out of jail, they began to plot their next move. Then one night they got a call. The house of one of their lawyers had been bombed! Luckily, no one was hurt. But the violence had gone too far.

JUMP —IN THE— THINK TANK

It took a lot of bravery to sit in at the lunch counters. Can you think of a time when you were brave?

Finally, the mayor said that the lunch counters should be desegregated. On May 10, 1960, Nashville lunch counters served Black customers for the first time. The protesters had won one battle, but there was still more to do.

Freedom Rides

The SNCC continued their protests around the South. They protested segregation in movie theaters and restaurants. Other organizations joined in, too. A group called the Congress of Racial Equality (CORE) reached out to John. They had a plan for a protest called the Freedom Rides. The Freedom Riders wanted to end segregation in bus stations. The waiting rooms and restrooms in bus stations in the South still didn't allow Black people. The law said they had to, but it was not usually **enforced**.

John traveled to Washington, DC, to meet the Freedom Riders, led by a man named James Farmer. The group spent weeks preparing for their protest. Then, on May 4, 1961, John and the rest of the protestors began their bus ride.

The Freedom Riders were a mixed group of Black and white people. Their plan was to go into bus station waiting spaces together. The law said they had the right to do that. They wanted to see if the law was being enforced.

At their first stop in the South, they tried to enter the station together. They were attacked. The riders kept going.

But a terrible thing happened. While John was away for a day, the Freedom Riders' bus was bombed. The riders escaped, only to be beaten by an angry mob. John worried about his friends. It could have been him on the bus!

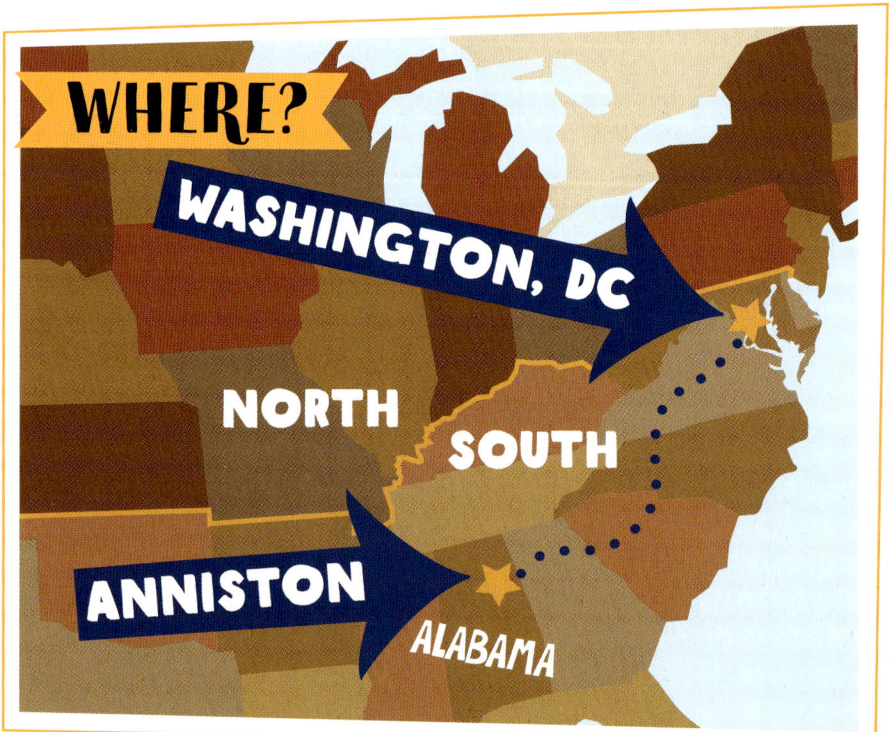

MYTH & FACT

MYTH: Random people attacked the Freedom Riders.

FACT: Attacks were often organized by members of the Ku Klux Klan (KKK), a **white supremacist** organization.

James Farmer called off the rides. It was too dangerous. But Diane Nash, a member of the SNCC, said no. Protestors like herself and John would never give up. They would continue to fight using nonviolence wherever they found injustice.

WHEN?

- John is arrested after a series of peaceful sit-ins. — FEBRUARY 27, **1960**
- John joins the Freedom Riders. — MAY 4, **1961**
- The Freedom Riders' bus is firebombed in Alabama. — MAY 14, **1961**

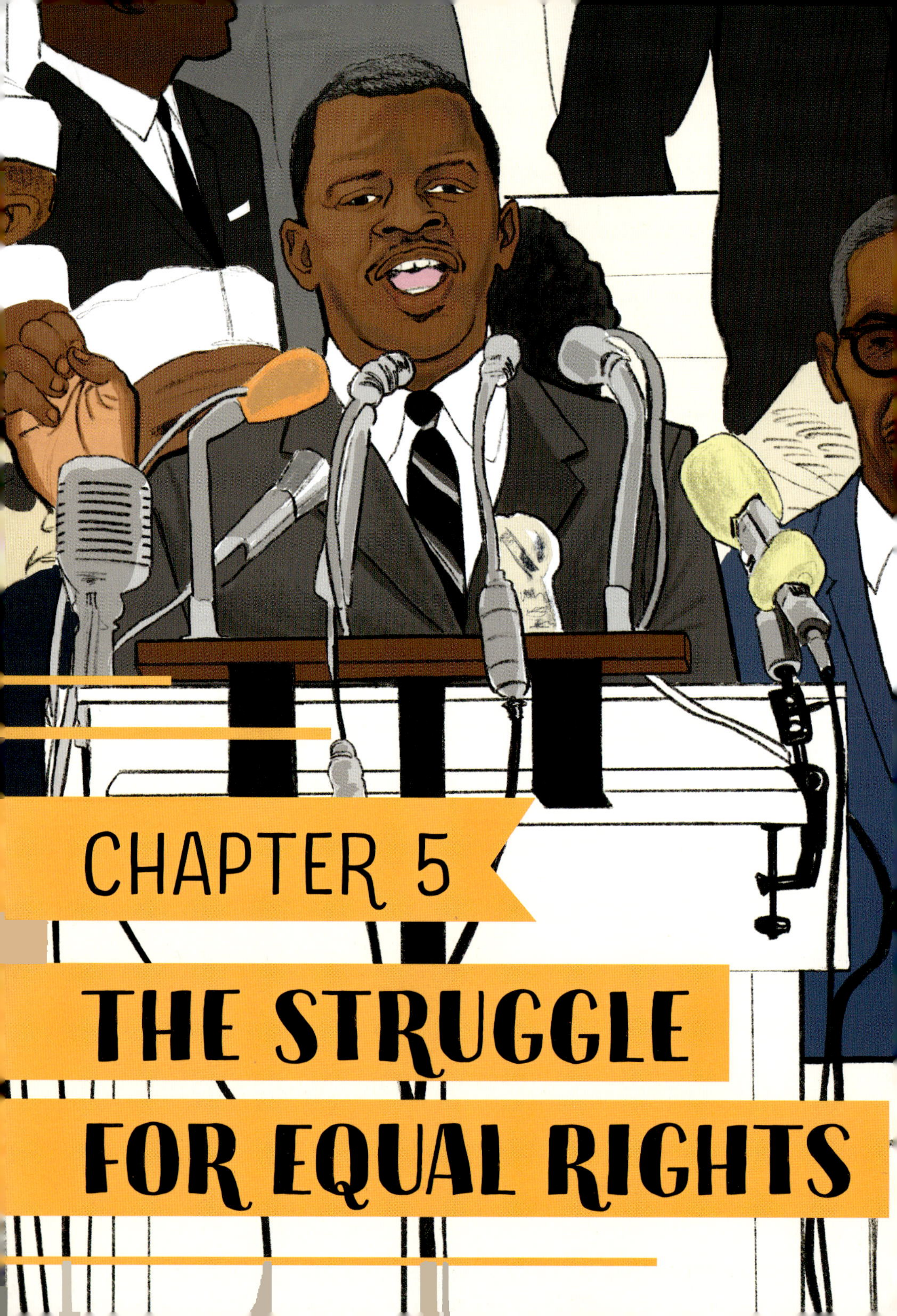

CHAPTER 5
THE STRUGGLE FOR EQUAL RIGHTS

March on Washington

The fight for equal rights continued. Protests were happening all across the South. Violence against peaceful protestors was caught on video and shown on the news. Many people were hurt, including children.

John escaped death several times. But he didn't let that stop him. He continued to peacefully protest. He was arrested 24 times. People saw that he was a leader. In 1963, he was asked to become **chairman** of the SNCC. John was just 23 years old. He felt emotional about all the violence in the country. He worried about his safety and the safety of his friends. Still, he agreed to lead the organization.

Later that year, an organizer named A. Philip Randolph came up with the idea of a march in support of jobs for Black Americans. He wanted to make a big statement. He asked five other

JUMP IN THE THINK TANK

Why is it important to be able to peacefully protest and march?

civil rights leaders for help: Martin Luther King Jr., James Farmer, Roy Wilkins, Whitney Young, and John. The group became known as the "Big Six." John was the youngest member.

The march was called the March on Washington for Jobs and Freedom. On August 28, 1963, about a quarter of a million people gathered under the Lincoln Memorial to hear the speakers. Dr. King delivered his famous "I Have a Dream" speech. Before Dr. King went on, John gave his own speech. At first he was nervous, but then he spoke strongly. He felt hopeful that things would change.

The good feelings didn't last long. Just two weeks later, a bomb in a Birmingham church killed four little girls. When Dr. King spoke at their funeral, 8,000 mourners came together.

Then in November, President John F. Kennedy was **assassinated**. It was a huge loss, and the country was in pain. Kennedy believed in equal rights for everyone. He had been working on a civil rights bill. The new president, Lyndon Johnson, followed his lead. The Civil Rights Act of 1964 passed the next year.

Bloody Sunday

John wanted to learn about how other Black people around the world were working to get equal rights. In 1964, he went to Africa to learn about how Black people there were struggling. Their fight was different, but there were many similarities. John learned a lot and felt ready to fight more in the United States.

He and the SNCC team decided to focus on voting rights next. Though Black people had the right to vote, it was very hard for them to register. Sometimes they had to take unfair tests.

Other times, they were met with threats and violence. John knew that until Black people could vote for leaders who would fight for them, nothing would change.

> "The **vote** is precious. It is almost sacred. It is the most powerful nonviolent tool we have in a **democracy**."

On March 7, 1965, John helped organize a march from Selma to Montgomery, Alabama. John knew he could get arrested. So, he prepared a backpack with a few things he might need in jail, like a book, a toothbrush and toothpaste, and an apple and orange. Dr. King was supposed to lead the march, but he was delayed, so John led it. They walked over the Edmund Pettus Bridge in Selma in a peaceful line. But the police were waiting on the other side.

The police attacked. The protestors were beaten with clubs and sprayed with tear gas. John was hit in the head and fell to the ground, bleeding. Meanwhile, reporters recorded what happened. The attack appeared on TV that night. This event became known as "Bloody Sunday." The videos caused the nation to respond.

After Bloody Sunday, leaders came to Selma to march. On March 21, Dr. King led about 25,000 protesters from Selma to Montgomery.

WHEN?

John speaks at the March on Washington.

AUGUST 28, 1963

Four girls are killed by a bomb at a church in Alabama.

SEPTEMBER 15, 1963

President John F. Kennedy is assassinated.

NOVEMBER 22, 1963

John was still healing from his injuries, but he marched, too. They walked 50 miles over five days. This time it worked. President Lyndon Johnson signed the Voting Rights Act of 1965 into law. Black voters' rights were now protected.

CHAPTER 6

ACTIVIST TO POLITICIAN

The New Way Forward

In 1966, John decided it was time to leave the SNCC. He was still committed to the civil rights movement, however. He went back to school. His life became all about studying and working. Then he met Lillian Miles at a New Year's Eve party. Lillian was a librarian at Atlanta University. She shared John's passion for civil rights, and they grew close.

Then Dr. King was assassinated on April 4, 1968. John was devastated. He had spent so much time working with Dr. King. His heart was broken. But, as always, he sprang into action. He put everything he had into the presidential campaign of Robert "Bobby" Kennedy. Bobby was running for president, just like his brother. People hoped that Bobby would take up the work his brother started. But the violence continued. On June 6, 1968, Bobby was assassinated, too.

> "Never, ever be afraid to make some **noise** and get in good trouble, necessary **trouble**."

John had seen so many of his friends and freedom fighters die. How much more could he take?

John decided that there had to be one good thing to happen in 1968. So, on December 21, 1968, he and Lillian were married. They welcomed a new year of hope together.

Congressman John Lewis

John and Lillian continued to fight for civil rights, and John continued his work on voter registration. In 1970, he took over as the director for the Voter Education Project. He helped register millions of voters! One of the first things he did was create a poster to inspire people. It showed two strong Black hands.

One hand was pulling cotton and the other was casting a ballot. It said, "Hands that pick cotton . . . now can pick our public officials." More than 10,000 posters were made and distributed throughout the South.

Meanwhile, his personal life was also beginning to change. In 1976, John and Lillian adopted their son, John-Miles Lewis. Then, John's friends and family asked him to consider taking on a new role. He had always fought for voters' rights. What if he was the person people could vote for?

In 1977, John ran to become a US congressman. He lost the election. Instead, he took on a new role. President Jimmy Carter appointed him to run a government program called ACTION. The program organized volunteers across the country. In 1981, John ran for a seat on the Atlanta city council and won. He held that seat until 1986. Then he decided to run for Congress again. This time he won!

JUMP IN THE THINK TANK

Even though John's life changed, he kept fighting for justice. How has your life changed? How has it stayed the same?

WHEN?

Dr. Martin Luther King Jr. is assassinated.

APRIL 4, **1968**

Robert Kennedy is assassinated.

JUNE 5, **1968**

John and Lillian marry.

DECEMBER 21, **1968**

John loses his first election.

APRIL 5, **1977**

John is elected to Atlanta's city council.

OCTOBER 7, **1981**

CHAPTER 7
WE SHALL OVERCOME SOMEDAY

☆ Equality for All People ☆

John Lewis was elected to Congress on November 4, 1986. He was reelected 16 times, serving almost 35 years! During that time, he continued to get into good trouble fighting for what's right. He led peaceful protests while in Congress. He even got arrested. In 2016, there was a deadly shooting in Florida. John was angry. He wanted Congress to pass laws that would make it harder for people to get guns. He protested by leading a 24-hour sit-in on the floor of Congress.

People began to recognize John for his important work. In 2001, he received the John F. Kennedy Profile in Courage Award for protecting the rights of all people. In 2011 he received the Presidential Medal of Freedom from Barack Obama. That's one of the highest honors an American can get!

Meanwhile, John wrote books about his life. He even wrote a graphic novel.

But it wasn't all celebrations for John. In 2012, he lost his beloved wife, Lillian. He was very sad, but he continued to work hard. In 2015, he led a march back across the bridge in Alabama where he almost lost his life. The march honored the 50th anniversary of Bloody Sunday. He reminded the crowd that it took three tries to get across the bridge before change happened.

> Every generation leaves behind a **legacy**. What that legacy will be is determined by the **people** of that generation. What legacy do you want to leave behind?

Then, in 2019, he got bad news. He had cancer. As usual, this didn't stop John. He decided he would fight cancer. He said, "I have been in some kind of fight—for freedom, equality, basic human rights—for nearly my entire life."

Spirit of Peace, Power of Love

In June of 2020, John made his last public appearance. He visited Black Lives Matter Plaza in Washington, DC. Protests had broken out across the United States after a Black man named George Floyd was killed by a police officer. John joined the protest. He wore a mask because the world was dealing with a deadly virus.

A few weeks later, John died on July 17, 2020. After he passed away, a newspaper published an essay he had written. It explained why he had been at the protests for George Floyd. He wrote, "I just had to see and feel it for myself that, after many years of silent witness, the truth is still marching on." He was honored in Washington, DC.

JUMP IN THE THINK TANK

John called fighting for what's right "good trouble." What do you think he meant by that? Can you think of an example of good trouble?

A double rainbow appeared in the sky the day before his funeral.

Many people came out to remember John Lewis at his funeral, even though the virus was still around. Everyone wore masks to stay safe. Three former presidents talked about working with him: Barack Obama, Bill Clinton, and George W. Bush. They told stories of all the good trouble he got into during his life. They talked about how important peace was to John. They even remembered his chickens! The youngest speaker was 12-year-old Tybre Faw. He had become friends with John two years earlier. He read one of John's favorite poems and said, "Let's honor him with getting in good trouble."

John's funeral took place in the church where Dr. King had been a pastor. Then his casket was taken across the Edmund Pettus Bridge one last time. A newspaper published his final words. He told people to vote and said, "Though I am gone, I urge you to answer the highest calling of your heart and stand up for what you truly believe."

WHEN?

John is elected to Congress.

NOVEMBER 4, 1986

John receives the JFK Profile in Courage Award.

MAY 5, 2001

John is awarded the Presidential Medal of Freedom.

FEBRUARY 15, 2011

John marches on the anniversary of Bloody Sunday.

MARCH 7, 2015

John passes away.

JULY 17, 2020

CHAPTER 8

SO...WHO WAS JOHN LEWIS?

Challenge Accepted!

You've learned all about John Lewis—a real American hero! Now, let's test your knowledge with a quick quiz. Try to answer these 10 questions without looking back in the book. Give it your best try!

1. John's family were:

- A Farmers
- B Store owners
- C Preachers
- D Protestors

2. Which city in Alabama was John born closest to?

- A Selma
- B Birmingham
- C Troy
- D Montgomery

3. What types of animals did John take care of on his childhood farm?

→ A Pigs
→ B Chickens
→ C Cows
→ D Goats

4. What job did John want when he was younger?

→ A Doctor
→ B Lawyer
→ C Preacher
→ D Singer

5. Which one of these actions ended segregation in schools?

→ A Lunch counter sit-ins
→ B The Voting Rights Act
→ C Bus strikes
→ D *Brown v. Board of Education*

6. What kind of protests did John take part in?

→ A Sit-ins
→ B Marches
→ C Freedom Rides
→ D All of the above

7. Who was **NOT** part of the Big Six group of activists?

→ A Roy Wilkins
→ B James Farmer
→ C Martin Luther King Jr.
→ D John F. Kennedy

8. Why did John and other protestors want to march from Selma to Montgomery?

→ A To show support for voting rights
→ B To desegregate schools
→ C To honor Martin Luther King Jr.
→ D To create new jobs

9. When did Bloody Sunday happen?

- A Last Saturday
- B July 17, 2020
- C March 7, 1965
- D February 21, 1940

10. How many times was John Lewis reelected to Congress?

- A 16 times
- B 35 times
- C Never
- D Only once

Answers: 1. A, 2. C, 3. B, 4. C, 5. D, 6. D, 7. D, 8. A, 9. C, 10. A

☆ Our World ☆

John Lewis was brave and courageous. He got in good trouble as a way to fight for change. His work made a difference in our lives today.

→ John Lewis believed in the power of nonviolent protests. He believed that seeing the human qualities in others is important and that violence is never the answer. His nonviolent protests helped end segregation and other unfair treatment.

→ John Lewis never gave up. He knew that sometimes change takes time. It took three marches through Selma and many protests for the voting rights bill to finally pass. There is still work to be done to make sure everyone is treated fairly. John's determination can help inspire us to keep pushing for change.

→ As a congressman, John continued to fight to change people's lives for the better. He helped pass laws to make sure that the civil rights movement is never forgotten.

JUMP IN THE THINK TANK FOR MORE!

→ During John's time, the TV played a big role in showing the world the violence peaceful protestors faced. These images led many people to action. How do videos inspire people today?

→ John believed that the right to vote was one of the most important rights. Why is it important for people to vote? What does voting do?

→ John wrote a graphic novel so that young people could know his story. Why do you think it was important for him to do that?

Glossary

acre: A measurement of land; one acre is 43,560 square feet of land

assassinate: To kill someone, usually a leader, by sudden or secret attack

Black: This word is capitalized when we talk about a group of people that shares an identity and community.

boycott: Refusal to deal with a person, store, or organization until certain conditions are met, agreed to, or both

chairman: A man who is in charge of a meeting or organization

civil rights: Basic rights that every person has under the laws of the government to be treated fairly and equally

congressman: A male member of the US House of Representatives

desegregate: To end laws, policies, or both that keep races apart such as at the movies, in school, or in a restaurant

enforce: To make people obey

enslaved: Forced to work without pay

equality: When every person in a group has the same rights and opportunities

harass: To trouble or bother

injustice: An act or behavior that's not fair, right, or equal

lunch counter: A place in a store where people can buy and eat food

nonviolence: Acting peacefully to bring about change

outraged: Angry at something unfair or wrong

pastor: A minister or priest in charge of a church

segregation: The separation of people, usually based on their race or skin color

sharecropping: A system in which landowners allow farmers to use land in exchange for part of their harvest

sit-in: A peaceful protest in which people refuse to leave a place until their demands are met

slavery: A system in which people are treated like property and forced to work against their will for no pay

white supremacism: A racist belief that white people are better than other people, including Black and Jewish people, often involving violence

Bibliography

Lewis, John. "Together, You Can Redeem the Soul of Our Nation." *New York Times*, July 30, 2020. NYTimes.com/2020/07/30/opinion/john-lewis-civil-rights-america.html.

Lewis, John, and Andrew Aydin. *March: Book One*. Marietta, GA: Top Shelf Productions, 2013.

———. *March: Book Two*. Marietta, GA: Top Shelf Productions, 2015.

———. *March: Book Three*. Marietta, GA: Top Shelf Productions, 2016.

Lewis, John, and Michael D'Orso. *Walking with the Wind: A Memoir of the Movement*. New York: Simon and Schuster, 1998.

Taylor, Derrick Bryson. "Who Were the Freedom Riders?" *New York Times*, July 18, 2020. NYTimes.com/2020/07/18/us/politics/freedom-riders-john-lewis-work.html.

About the Author

TONYA LESLIE, PhD, is an educator, keynote speaker, and researcher. She studies issues related to educational equity and literacy. She is also a writer. Her other children's books include *So Other People Would Be Also Free: The Real Story of Rosa Parks for Kids* and *The Story of Barack Obama*. Tonya splits her time between New York City and Belize, Central America. She enjoys visiting museums, swimming, and reading on airplanes. Learn more about her work at TonyaLeslie.com.

About the Illustrator

JERRARD K. POLK was born and raised in Charlotte, North Carolina. Jerrard got his professional start at the age of 15 as a caricature artist at parties and events. He went on to study graphic design at the Art Institute of Charlotte, and later attended the Illustration Academy at Ringling College of Art and Design. Having spent many years of his adult life in Bermuda, Jerrard's art is inspired by the natural beauty, bright pastel colors, and sharp lines created by the island's ever-present sun. He is also inspired by jazz and the dapper fashion of its innovators. He loves telling little-known stories of everyday people to encourage children from all cultures. Jerrard now lives in the tranquil countryside of upstate New York with his wife and son.

WHO WILL INSPIRE YOU NEXT?

EXPLORE A WORLD OF HEROES AND ROLE MODELS IN ***THE STORY OF...*** BIOGRAPHY SERIES FOR NEW READERS.

LOOK FOR THIS SERIES
WHEREVER BOOKS AND EBOOKS ARE SOLD

Alexander Hamilton
Albert Einstein
Frida Kahlo
George Washington
Jane Goodall
Ruth Bader Ginsburg
Helen Keller
Marie Curie